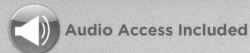

CLASSIC ROCK FOR VIOLIN

Audio Access Included

Visit **www.halleonard.com/mylibrary**

Enter Code

6383-1213-1645-9967

Audio Arrangements by Peter Deneff
Tracking, mixing, and mastering by BeatHouse Music

ISBN 978-1-4803-5453-1

7777 W. BLUEMOUND RD. P.O. BOX 13819 MILWAUKEE, WI 53213

Visit Hal Leonard Online at
www.halleonard.com

CONTENTS

ANOTHER ONE BITES THE DUST

Words and Music by
JOHN DEACON

BORN TO BE WILD

Words and Music by
MARS BONFIRE

6

BROWN EYED GIRL

WordsWords and Music by
VAN MORRISON

EVERY BREATH YOU TAKE

Words and Music by
STING

8

DUST IN THE WIND

Words and Music by
KERRY LIVGREN

FLY LIKE AN EAGLE

Words and Music by
STEVE MILLER

UP AROUND THE BEND

Words and Music by
JOHN FOGERTY

I HEARD IT THROUGH THE GRAPEVINE

Words and Music by NORMAN J. WHITFIELD
amd BARRETT STRONG

I SHOT THE SHERIFF

Words and Music by
BOB MARLEY

OYE COMO VA

Words and Music by
TITO PUENTE